THE FUTURE IS FEMALE

ALTERNATOR BOOKS™

Changemakers in
SPORTS

Women Leading the Way

NGERI NNACHI

Lerner Publications ◆ Minneap

I dedicate this book to every girl who uses her body in admirable ways and makes magic every single day while doing so!

Lerner Publications Company
An imprint of Lerner Publishing Group, Inc.
241 First Avenue North
Minneapolis, MN 55401 USA

For reading levels and more information, look up this title at www.lernerbooks.com.

Main body text set in Aptifer Sans LT Pro Medium.
Typeface provided by Linotype AG.

Editor: Brianna Kaiser **Designer:** Athena Currier
Lerner team: Martha Kranes

Library of Congress Cataloging-in-Publication Data

Names: Nnachi, Ngeri, author.
Title: Changemakers in sports : women leading the way / Ngeri Nnachi.
Description: Minneapolis, MN : Lerner Publications, [2024] | Series: Alternator books. The future is female | Includes bibliographical references and index. | Audience: Ages 8–12 | Audience: Grades 4–6 | Summary: "Dive into this exciting book about women making change in the world of sports. From past and present stars, readers will love learning about the accomplishments of amazing athletes in a wide variety of sports"— Provided by publisher.
Identifiers: LCCN 2023010613 (print) | LCCN 2023010614 (ebook) | ISBN 9798765608890 (library binding) | ISBN 9798765625033 (paperback) | ISBN 9798765618424 (epub)
Subjects: LCSH: Women athletes—United States—Biography—Juvenile literature. | BISAC: JUVENILE NONFICTION / Biography & Autobiography / Women
Classification: LCC GV697.A1 N66 2024 (print) | LCC GV697.A1 (ebook) | DDC 796.092/52 [B]—dc23/eng/20230308

LC record available at https://lccn.loc.gov/2023010613
LC ebook record available at https://lccn.loc.gov/2023010614

Manufactured in the United States of America
1-1009551-51567-6/6/2023

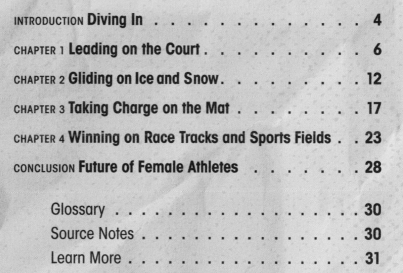

Table of Contents

INTRODUCTION

Diving In

On September 3, 2021, Jessica Long dove into the pool at the Paralympics in Tokyo, Japan. The Paralympics are an international competition for athletes with physical disabilities. Less than 20 seconds into the 100-meter butterfly race, she took the lead and stayed there. She finished the race at 1:09:87 to take the gold medal. It was her 16th Paralympic gold medal.

Long swam in her first Paralympics in 2004 at twelve years old. Since then, she has won 29 Paralympic medals. She has won the second most Paralympic medals in US history.

In 2021 Jessica Long wins her sixteenth Paralympic gold medal.

Women have been leading the way in sports for decades. Although not all amazing women athletes can be included in this book, the athletes mentioned here are among the women making waves in many sports.

CHAPTER 1

Leading on the Court

The Women's Tennis Association (WTA), the pro women's tennis league, started in 1973.

The first pro women's basketball league, the Women's National Basketball Association (WNBA), began play in 1997. Since then, women have been making names for themselves on and off the tennis and basketball courts.

The Golden Slam

Serena Williams is known to many as tennis's G.O.A.T. (greatest of all time). She turned pro in 1995 at 14 years

Serena Williams celebrates winning the 2013 French Open.

old. At the US Open four years later, she won her first major singles title.

Williams won 23 major singles titles and 14 major doubles titles. She also won four Olympic gold medals—one in singles and three in doubles. Because she won all four majors and Olympic gold medals, Williams earned career Golden Slams. She is the only player to have earned a career Golden Slam in

> **"I really think a champion is defined not by their wins but by how they can recover when they fall."**
>
> —SERENA WILLIAMS, 2012

both singles and doubles. In 2022 Williams announced that she would be stepping down from tennis to focus on other things in her life.

Back-to-Back Titles

At the 2018 US Open, 20-year-old Naomi Osaka shocked the world when she beat Serena Williams to win the major. Then,

Naomi Osaka playing in the 2018 US Open

at the 2019 Australian Open, she won again. It was her second major title in a row. Osaka again won the US Open in 2020 and the Australian Open in 2021.

In 2021 Osaka removed herself from some tournaments to focus on her mental health. On and off the court, she works to bring more awareness to mental health.

Phoenix Mercury All-Star

Diana Taurasi is one of the greatest basketball players of all time. The Phoenix Mercury selected her with the first overall pick in the 2004 WNBA draft. She helped the team win the WNBA Finals in 2007, 2009, and 2014. She has also helped Team USA win five Olympic gold medals.

Taurasi has been selected to 10 WNBA All-Star Games. The game is played each year

Diana Taurasi heads down the court during the 2014 WNBA All-Star Game.

HITTING THE BALL

Lauren Schad of the Cheyenne River Lakota Nation was a top college volleyball player at the University of San Diego. She went on to play five seasons of pro volleyball for a team in France and helped the team win major championships. She retired in 2022.

Lauren Schad playing in a 2019 match in France

between the best players of the WNBA's Western and Eastern Conferences. Taurasi has also been named to 14 All-WNBA teams. The honor is given to the best WNBA players following each season.

Lisa Leslie (*holding the ball*) plays for Team USA during a game in 1994.

First Slam Dunk

Lisa Leslie helped Team USA win four Olympic gold medals and the Los Angeles Sparks win the WNBA Finals in 2001 and 2002. In 2002 she slammed the first dunk in the WNBA and became the first WNBA player to score 3,000 career points. Because of her many accomplishments, she is one of the greatest WNBA players of all time.

Leslie retired from playing in 2009. Off the court, she has starred as herself in many movies and television shows. Leslie is the head coach of the Triplets in the BIG3, a 3-on-3 pro basketball league, and a sports analyst.

CHAPTER 2

Gliding on Ice and Snow

Every year, women are tackling winter sports.
They are breaking records, winning medals, and more.

A Skiing Champion

Mikaela Shiffrin is a record-breaking alpine skier. Alpine skiing is skiing downhill. Shiffrin won a gold medal at the 2014 Olympics and a gold and a silver medal at the 2018 Olympics.

Shiffrin won her first World Cup race at 17 years old and has been the Overall World Cup champion five times. In 2023

Mikaela Shiffrin competes in a World Cup alpine skiing race in 2013.

she won her seventh world championship gold medal. That year, she also won her 88th World Cup, breaking the record of most World Cup wins of any alpine skier.

Michelle Kwan won a bronze medal for her performance in the 2002 Olympics.

Top Figure Skater

Michelle Kwan is the most decorated US figure skater. She won her first competition at seven years old. At the 1995 World Championships, she took gold. One year later, she won both the US and World Championships. She won the World Championships five times and the US Championships a record-tying nine times.

"Learn from your mistakes to keep growing. Work hard for yourself and have fun."

—MICHELLE KWAN, 2017

SUPER SNOWBOARDER

In 2018, 17-year-old snowboarder Chloe Kim won her first Olympic gold medal. She won another gold medal at the 2022 Olympics in Beijing, China.

Chloe Kim celebrating her gold medal win at the 2022 Olympics

Kwan went on to study international relations. She has worked in different government jobs. For over a decade, Kwan has also supported the Special Olympics—an international competition for athletes with intellectual disabilities.

Eileen Gu holds her gold medal at the 2022 Olympics.

The Triple Threat

Eileen Gu is a freestyle skier. At 18 Gu became the first woman to land a forward double cork 1440—a jump where she flipped twice in the air while spinning four times.

Gu became the youngest Olympic champion in freestyle skiing after winning two gold medals and one silver at the 2022 Olympics in Beijing, China. The wins made her the first freestyle athlete to win three medals at a single Olympics. Gu was the third-highest-paid female athlete in the world in 2022.

CHAPTER 3

Taking Charge on the Mat

Multiple sports use a mat. Whether an athlete is flipping their own body or someone else's body, they are making change on the mat of their sports.

A Wrestling First

Mary Lillian Ellison, known in the ring as the Fabulous Moolah, holds the record as the longest-reigning women's world champion in wrestling. She is a four-time winner of the World Wrestling Entertainment (WWE) Women's Championship.

Ellison became the first woman allowed to wrestle at Madison Square Garden, an arena in New York City. In 1995 she became the first woman to join the WWE Hall of Fame. Four years later, she became the oldest champion in the history of pro wrestling. She was 76 years old.

Mary Lillian Ellison competes in a pro wrestling event in 1986.

Ronda Rousey celebrates winning a 2015 UFC event.

Mixed Martial Artist

Ronda Rousey is a wrestler and mixed martial artist. In the 2008 Olympics, Rousey became the first American woman to earn an Olympic medal in judo, a kind of martial art. She officially became a mixed martial artist in 2011.

Rousey held the record for most Ultimate Fighting Championship (UFC) title defenses by a woman until Valentina Shevchenko broke the record in 2022. Rousey retired from mixed martial arts in 2016 and in 2018, she became the first female fighter to join the UFC Hall of Fame. Following her retirement, she began a career in pro wrestling with WWE.

THE DANCING GYMNAST

In 2016 Laurie Hernandez helped Team USA win the gold medal at the Olympic Games in Rio de Janeiro, Brazil. She also won a silver medal in the individual events. Later that year, the 16-year-old was on the dancing competition show *Dancing with the Stars*. She became the youngest person to win the competition.

Laurie Hernandez flips on the balance beam at the 2016 Olympics.

"No matter what race or color you are, you can aspire to do something great."

—LAURIE HERNANDEZ, 2016

Simone Biles holding her gold medals at the 2019 World Championships

Gymnastics's G.O.A.T.

Simone Biles is often called gymnastics's G.O.A.T. Biles was the first woman to win three World Championships all-around titles in a row and the first American woman to win seven all-around titles at the US Gymnastics Championships.

Biles is the most decorated American gymnast. She has won 32 medals at the World Championships, 19 of them gold. And she has won seven Olympic medals, four of them gold. Off the mat, Biles brings awareness to mental health. In 2022 President Joe Biden awarded her the Presidential Medal of Freedom, an award given for making great contributions to society.

A GOLD FIRST

In 2021 at the Olympics in Tokyo, Japan, Sunisa Lee won the gold medal in the all-around event. Lee became the first Hmong American to win a gold medal.

Sunisa Lee competes in the floor exercise event at the Tokyo Olymipcs in 2021.

CHAPTER 4

Winning on Race Tracks and Sports Fields

From track-and-field events to soccer competitions, many women athletes are making great achievements.

A Speedy Sight

Florence Griffith Joyner, also called Flo Jo, is known as the fastest woman of all time. At the 1988 Olympic Trials, Joyner broke the world record for the 100-meter, finishing the race at 10.49 seconds.

Florence Griffith Joyner running in an
event at the 1988 Olympics

Joyner did even better at the 1988 Olympics in Seoul,
South Korea. She won three gold medals and one silver. In
the 200-meter, Joyner broke another world record when she
finished the race at 21.34 seconds. Both of Joyner's records
have yet to be passed. She joined the National Track and Field
Hall of Fame in 1995.

Top-Ranked Golfer

Paula Creamer started playing golf at the age of 10. By 13 she was already a top-ranked girls junior golfer. Before turning pro, Paula won 19 tournaments and became the top-ranked girls player of the American Junior Golf Association in 2003.

Paula Creamer wins the 2010 US Women's Open.

INSIDE THE USWNT

The US Women's National Soccer Team (USWNT) began in 1985. The team has won four Olympic gold medals (1996, 2004, 2008, and 2012) and four Fédération Internationale de Football Association (FIFA) Women's World Cups (1991, 1999, 2015, and 2019).

Players of the USWNT celebrate after winning the 2015 FIFA Women's World Cup.

Creamer joined the Ladies Professional Golf Association (LPGA) in 2005. That year the 18-year-old won her first LPGA event—the Sybase Classic. The win made her the youngest player to ever win a multi-round LPGA event. Creamer has won 10 LPGA Tour events, including the 2010 US Women's Open.

Sophia Smith Playing for the Portland Thorns in 2022

A Star Forward

Sophia Smith is a star forward. She played on US national teams for players under 23 years old. She also helped her team at Stanford University win the National Collegiate Athletic Association (NCAA) Championship in 2019. In 2020 the Portland Thorns of the National Women's Soccer League (NWSL) picked Smith to join the team.

Smith had an incredible season in 2022. She finished the year as the leading scorer for the Portland Thorns and the USWNT. She was also named the NWSL Most Valuable Player and the US Soccer Female Player of the Year.

CONCLUSION

Future of Female Athletes

The Women's Sports Foundation was founded in 1974 by tennis star Billie Jean King to provide girls access to sports. Since then, women have continued to make strides in sports while honoring the many women that paved the way before them. What sports do you like? You can make strides in sports too!

Billie Jean King gives a speech for the Women's Sports Foundation in 2004.

Glossary

career Golden Slam: winning all four majors (the Australian Open, the French Open, Wimbledon, and the US Open) and an Olympic gold medal

decorated: an athlete who has won one or more medals

disability: a physical or mental condition that makes it more difficult to do certain activities

doubles: tennis matches with two players on each side

draft: a yearly event where teams take turns choosing new players

freestyle: a sporting event with fewer restrictions on moves or styles

mental health: the degree of health of one's mind and emotions

mixed martial arts: a combat sport that includes boxing, wrestling, karate, and judo techniques

retire: to end a job or career

singles: tennis matches with one player on each side

sports analyst: a person who looks at the techniques and performance of an athlete

Source Notes

8   Ahmed Rizvi, "The Fall and Rise of Maturing Serena Williams," *National*, September 9, 2012, https://www.thenationalnews.com/sport/the-fall-and-rise-of-maturing-serena-williams-1.632294.

14   Jim Clash, "Michelle Kwan Says Yes to Kids and the Old 6.0 Skate Judging System," *Forbes*, May 7, 2017, https://www.forbes.com/sites /jimclash/2017/03/07/michelle-kwan-says-yes-to-kids-and-the-old -6-0-skate-judging-system/?sh=4284f6386336.

20   "This 16-Year-Old Gymnast Is Doing Hispanics Proud," *Time*, November 8, 2016, https://time.com/4555468/laurie-hernandez-american-voices/.

Learn More

Britannica Kids: Winter Sports
https://kids.britannica.com/students/article/winter-sports/277771

Fishman, Jon M. *Tennis's G.O.A.T.: Serena Williams, Roger Federer, and More*. Minneapolis: Lerner Publications, 2022.

Greatest Female Athletes of All Time
https://www.cbsnews.com/pictures/greatest-female-athletes-of-all-time/

Kane, Bryce. *Top Teams in Women's Soccer*. Broomall, PA: Mason Crest, 2019.

Llanas, Sheila Griffin. *Women in Track and Field*. Lake Elmo, MN: Focus Readers, 2020.

Nicks, Erin. *Best Female Gymnasts of All Time*. Minneapolis: SportsZone, 2021.

Sports Illustrated Kids
https://www.sikids.com

Women's Sports Foundation
https://www.womenssportsfoundation.org

Index

Photo Acknowledgments

Lintao Zhang/Getty Images, p. 5; Julian Finney/Getty Images, p. 7; Tim Clayton/Corbis/Getty Images, p. 8; Christian Petersen/Getty Images, p. 9; Eddy Lemaistre/Icon Sport/Getty Images, p. 10; Bob Stowell/Getty Images, p. 11; Alexis Boichard/Agence Zoom/Getty Images, p. 13; Popperfoto/Getty Images, p. 14; Mao Jianjun/China News Service/Getty Images, p. 15; VCG/Getty Images, p. 16; Paul Natkin/Getty Images, p. 18; Jeff Bottari/Zuffa LLC/Getty Images, p. 19; Lars Baron/Getty Images, p. 20; Laurence Griffiths/Getty Images, p. 21; Jamie Squire/Getty Images, p. 22; Tony Duffy/Allsport/Getty Images, p. 24; Chris Graythen/Getty Images, p. 25; Jose Breton/NurPhoto/Getty Images, p. 26; Brad Smith/ISI Photos/Getty Images, p. 27; Peter Kramer/Getty Images, p. 29.

Design Elements: Old Man Stocker/Shutterstock, p. 1; MPFphotography/Shutterstock, p. 1; schab/Shutterstock, p. 1.

Cover: AP Photo/Pavel Bednyakov/Sputnik, (Eileen Gu); AP Photo/Jae C. Hong, (Jessica Long); AP Photo/Michel Spingler, (Serena Williams).